Raising Healthy, Happy, Cooperative Kids

Discover the root cause of all disruptive and defiant behavior disorders like ADHD and Oppositional Defiant Disorder, AND the magic formula to gain cooperation — even with the most severe cases.

Copyright © 2018 Bonnie & Thomas Liotta

All rights reserved. No portion of this book may be reproduced, stored in a retrieval system, or transmitted in any form or by any means - electronic, mechanical, photocopy, recording, scanning, or other - except for brief quotations in critical reviews or articles, without the prior written permission of the author.

Disclaimer: The information in this book was correct at the time of publication but the author does not assume any liability for loss or damage caused by errors or omissions. This book is written from our perspective. We have represented events as faithfully as possible.

For speaking inquiries, permission requests, and bulk order purchase options, contact:

support@creatingchampionsforlife.com

Bonnie & Thomas Liotta
701 5th Ave. Ste 4200
Seattle WA 98104
https://www.creatingchampionsforlife.com/

~Dedication~

This book is dedicated to:

The **champion** who resides in the heart of every child.

The **teachers and leaders** in our lives who gave us the courage to pursue our passion and purpose of helping all children know their greatness by the time they are 12 (although it's NEVER too late)...

Our **children,** Jacob, Kyra, Jennie and Zachary, for giving us a reason to persevere. Your future is the reason for our drive today. Your future is our reason.

~ Prologue ~

Champion: Someone who is highly skilled in any area of life.

Synonyms: ace, adept, genius, hotshot, maven, mavin, sensation, star, superstar, virtuoso, whiz, whizz, wiz, wizard.

Inside the spirit of every newborn lies the heart of either a cheat or a champion, a loser or a winner, a victim or a victor. How you choose to parent your child will be the difference between the dread of parenting hell or the joy of parenting heaven.

Have you not imagined peaceful, joy-filled days, enjoying fun and laughter with your children?

Hi, I'm Bonnie Liotta! I have been exactly where you are now — living in a toxic nightmare with my children. I found myself secretly crying in the bathroom. My dream of being a patient and loving parent was crushed and gone!

I was hopeless.

In 2011, three of my four children had been diagnosed with attention deficit hyperactivity disorder (ADHD). My youngest was also diagnosed with oppositional defiant disorder (ODD). I did not know I was the leading cause of their disorders; that I was hurting them with how I was parenting, not physically but emotionally, mentally and spiritually.

In the depths of my darkest hour as a parent, the answer came to me through a miraculous series of events.

In 2011, I found the answers I had been praying for when it comes to winning as a parent. I saw for myself the most fantastic way to empower all children to their true champion selves!

At the same time, I discovered a lie so big it would affect the entire world in my search for answers, even though most of us weren't even born yet. All of a sudden, I could see the solutions to remove all children from the spectrum of child labels and the hidden parent trap beyond a shadow of a doubt!

Here is the great news and our promise to you, Mom and Dad: YOU have ALL the power to help your child or teenager transform from child behavior disorder diagnoses, constant disrespect and disruptive, defiant behavior to healthy, happy, cooperative kids!

Yes, you do! We are going to help you see it inside the pages of this inspiring and life-changing book!

Table of Contents

CHAPTER 1
Introduction 1

CHAPTER 2
Imperative Message from Our Kids 9

CHAPTER 3
Potential of a Child 19

CHAPTER 4
ADHD~21st Century Pandemic Child Disorder 27

CHAPTER 5
Your Role 37

CHAPTER 6
The Goal 49

CHAPTER 7
Win-Win Plan 55

CHAPTER 8
Guiding Behavior 69

CHAPTER 9
Desire 77

CHAPTER 10
Creature of Habit 83

CHAPTER 11
Parent Paradise 89

CHAPTER 12
New Beginning 97

CHAPTER 1

Introduction

Babies are born with zero habits and have pure potential to be, do or have anything you are willing to teach them.

This simple-to-read but profoundly influential book aims to help you expand your perspective on how to raise your children the right way. We believe the information we have provided will help you build a solid foundation of understanding to create authentic, positive change for you and your children.
You will be introduced to concepts and strategies that you have never heard or thought of before, your imagination will be stretched, and you will finally have a formula that works to promote cooperation. That all being said, this book may be easy to read, but it's not for the weak-minded!

This book IS for you if:
- you can feel in your heart that there is a better way.
- you are ready to learn how to communicate with your child in a way that produces harmony and cooperation.
- you want a natural solution to help your children become empowered and happy.
- you are willing to change a few beliefs about child behavior disorders.
- how you choose to parent is open to exploration.

This book ISN'T for you if:
- You are choosing to hang on to the alibis and excuses created for the immediate gratification of parents.
- You choose to see nothing else but that there is something wrong with your child that only a doctor can fix.
- You are seeking an easy way out or a quick fix for your child's outrageous behavior.

No matter how chaotic things may seem right now, you will soon see that all babies are born with zero habits. Every child has the pure potential to be, do or have anything. Are you are willing to teach them — consciously?

No one wants to parent a child who ends up living an unhappy, desperate adult life… Still, it is happening right now on a vast, disturbing and heart-wrenching scale. You only have one chance to raise your precious babies. You have 18 years to prepare them for the world out there.

One day you are ecstatic, rocking your sweet baby to sleep in your arms. The next thing you know, he is running around the house screaming and causing mischief like a bull in a china shop. Before you know it, your baby will be an adult living a life filled with adversity and challenges.

They will either grow up to be a productive leader able to overcome or a demanding victim to their circumstances. Which direction do you think frustration, confusion, anger and punishment-oriented parenting will take your child in? You are right, the demanding victim's direction!

Wouldn't you love your children to grow up knowing they can overcome adversities no matter what they choose and what challenges they face?

> *"The future belongs to those who believe in the beauty of their dreams." — Eleanor Roosevelt*

Science will show you that we create our destinies by how we approach and react to circumstances. What are you teaching your children about how the world works?

By the time you complete this short but powerful book, Raising Healthy, Happy, Cooperative Kids, you will understand the most significant mistakes "parenting experts" have been teaching for nearly a century now. Whether these experts are aware or unaware of these parenting blunders does not matter.

You will see these mistakes are sadly leading teenagers who:

- feel unworthy;
- do not like themselves;
- believe something is wrong with them;
- have no drive or purpose;
- become drug addicts; and
- believe suicide and trauma are the only ways for their lives to have meaning.

You're going to learn:

- exactly what child behavior disorders like ADHD and ODD are, so you can champion for your children;

- the cause of child mental and behavior disorders so you can believe in your child's potential and avoid the spectrum;
- the solution that will help you help your child authentically develop the necessary life skills for perfect mental health;
- why your child is angry and self-conscious — even though you know he's loved beyond measure;
- how to help your child go through life with more confidence and joy;
- how to authentically motivate your child to listen to your requests and engage in life;
- what will inspire your children to put forth effort on homework and chores;
- to help your child develop new solution-oriented thought patterns to become more independent; and
- exactly what to do now to begin a positive transformation.

Yes, it is possible to help your children become all you dream they can be! They can be motivated. They can learn. They can cooperate. They can… do anything you are willing to teach them how to do!

Every child is indeed different, just like how plants vary from one another. A rose is different from a tulip, for instance. However, the fact remains that both a rose and tulip require water and sunlight to survive.

We have been taught that a timeout may and may not work with a certain child. But, we know for sure that all children respond to a smile, praise, and proactive plans with enthusiasm. Every child will feel important and loved when validated and will respond poorly to being told "no," "that's bad," "don't," or "you can't."

Thomas Liotta is the only person on the planet who decided back in 1994 to provide a 100% proof to the previous statements. It was a decision that would later affect millions of families worldwide, most of whom don't even exist yet. It was a decision that would inevitably change the destiny of humanity for the better.

To empower thousands of students enrolled in Modoo Hana TKD Academy in Seatac, WA, Thomas developed an incredible formula that works to engage and motivate kids. He perfected his strategies over 15 years that hundreds of moms showed up at his school asking, "Can you please fix my kid?"

Thomas' school was licensed as a non-profit and the only alternative to traditional daycare. Because of this, his school attracted many students who had been asked to leave their existing childcare due to behavioral issues. These were some of the most outrageously behaved children in the Seattle area.

His was the only school permitted to visit the local fire department because his students always left the Firehall cleaner than before they arrived. They even brought birthday cake! He could have his students walk in single file line, hands at their sides for however long requested. You can do it too!

You are about to embark on an exciting adventure of struggle, betrayal and hope! Some of what you will learn inside the following few pages will mortify you. And by the time you reach the end, you will realize that you have found the answer to your parenting prayers: the recipe for raising healthy, happy, cooperative kids!

Yes, all personalities are unique. Like gravity, the law of cause and effect applies to every individual. This means that every thought, word and action will create an inevitable reaction or effect. There will be differences in how your children react.

Do you want to know the cause so you can genuinely transform your present parent-child relationship? Do you desire it badly enough to read this book to the end? The choice is yours!

If you're ready, let us get started.

CHAPTER 2

Imperative Message from Our Kids

"Parents all over the globe are struggling unnecessarily with the behavior of their children."

We hear complaints of constant anger, arguing and frustration silently residing inside homes from parents around the globe. The toxic and dark environment that we have been taught to create in our homes and classrooms through parenting books, articles and videos are not just frustrating; it's downright frightening!

Did you know that:
- ADHD and other child behavior and mood disorders, including anxiety and depression, have increased to the tune of more than 54% of today's youth being prescribed medication as a solution;
- teenage suicide is the number one cause of adolescent death worldwide; and
- school gun shootings done by children's classmates have increased by 300% in the last few decades?

Did you know that school gun massacres began just decades ago? The Thurston High School shooting, for instance, occurred on May 21, 1998, in Springfield, Oregon. The perpetrator was a 15-year-old freshman student, Kipland Kinkel, who had been scheduled to appear at an expulsion hearing the day before he murdered his parents, killed two of his classmates and wounded 25 others.

Only a year later, the Columbine High School massacre took place. This was a school shooting and attempted bombing on April 20, 1999, in Columbine, Colorado, United States by two 12th-grade students, Eric Harris and Dylan Klebold who murdered 12 students and one teacher.

Until Columbine, most school-related shootings were specific, like a particular teacher, girlfriend or bully, with two to ten episodes a year. In 2008, school shootings broke ten a year to 11, 26 in 2013, and 35 in

2014. Fast forward to 2018 — there are 23 school shooting incidents so far!

When I try to contemplate about these massacres happening constantly, I get to see that when God wants you to learn a lesson, you will initially experience a little pain, then a bit more — until eventually, you are hit in the head with a BIG brick!
The brick is hitting us in the head, moms and dads. Children need us to step up... now!

The Thurston and Columbine school shooting incidents were just two of the HUNDREDS of shooting massacres that have happened and are still happening today. I have provided here a list of schools where shooting massacres occurred, committed by students themselves:

Thurston High School.
Columbine High School.
Heritage High School.
Deming Middle School.
Fort Gibson Middle School.
Buell Elementary School.
Lake Worth Middle School.
University of Arkansas.
Junipero Serra High School.
Santana High School.
Bishop Neumann High School.
Pacific Lutheran University.
Granite Hills High School.
Low Wallace High School.
Martin Luther King, Jr. High School.
Appalachian School of Law.
Washington High School.
Conception Abbey.
Benjamin Tasker Middle School.
University of Arizona.
Lincoln High School.
John McDonogh High School.
Red Lion Area Junior High School.
Case Western Reserve University.
Rocori High School.
Ballou High School.

Randallstown High School.

Bowen High School.

Red Lake Senior High School.

Harlan Community Academy High School.

Campbell County High School.

Milwee Middle School.

Roseburg High School.

Pine Middle School.

Essex Elementary School.

Duquesne University.

Platte Canyon High School.

Weston High School.

West Nickel Mines School.

Joplin Memorial Middle School.

Henry Foss High School.

Compton Centennial High School.

Virginia Tech.

Success Tech Academy.

Miami Carol City Senior High School.

Hamilton High School.

Louisiana Technical College.

Mitchell High School.

E.O. Green Junior High School.

Northern Illinois University.

Lakota Middle School.

Knoxville Central High School.

Willoughby South High School.

Henry Ford High School.

University of Central Arkansas.

Dillard High School.

Dunbar High School.

Hampton University.

Harvard College.

Larose-Cut Off Middle School.

International Studies Academy.

Skyline College.

Discovery Middle School.

University of Alabama.

DeKalb School.

Deer Creek Middle School.

Ohio State University.

Mumford High School.

University of Texas.

Kelly Elementary School.

Marinette High School.

Aurora Central High School.

Millard South High School.

Martinsville West Middle School.

Worthing High School.

Millard South High School.

Highlands Intermediate School.

Cape Fear High School.

Chardon High School.

Episcopal School of Jacksonville.

Oikos University.

Hamilton High School.

Perry Hall School.

Normal Community High School.

University of South Alabama.

Banner Academy South.

University of Southern California.

Sandy Hook Elementary School.

Apostolic Revival Center Christian School.

Taft Union High School.

Osborn High School.

Stevens Institute of Business and Arts.

Hazard Community and Technical College.

Chicago State University.

Lone Star College-North.

Cesar Chavez High School.

Price Middle School.

University of Central Florida.

New River Community College.

Grambling State University.

Massachusetts Institute of Technology.

Ossie Ware Mitchell Middle School.

Ronald E. McNair Discovery Academy.

North Panola High School.

Carver High School.

Agape Christian Academy.

Sparks Middle School.

North Carolina A&T State University.

Stephenson High School.

Brashear High School.

West Orange High School.

Arapahoe High School.

Edison High School.

Liberty Technology Magnet High School.

Hillhouse High School.

Berrendo Middle School.

Purdue University.

South Carolina State University.

Los Angeles Valley College.

Charles F. Brush High School.

University of Southern California.

Georgia Regents University.

Academy of Knowledge Preschool.

Benjamin Banneker High School.

D. H. Conley High School.

East English Village Preparatory Academy.

Paine College.

Georgia Gwinnett College.

John F. Kennedy High School.

Seattle Pacific University.

Reynolds High School.

Indiana State University.

Albemarle High School.

Fern Creek Traditional High School.

Langston Hughes High School.

Marysville Pilchuck High School.

Florida State University.

Miami Carol City High School.

Rogers State University.

Rosemary Anderson High School.

Wisconsin Lutheran High School.

Frederick High School.

Tenaya Middle School.

Bethune-Cookman University.

Pershing Elementary School.

Wayne Community College.

J.B. Martin Middle School.

Southwestern Classical Academy.

Savannah State University.

Harrisburg High School.

Umpqua Community College.

Northern Arizona University.

Texas Southern University.

Tennessee State University.

Winston-Salem State University.

Mojave High School.

Lawrence Central High School.

Franklin High School.

Muskegon Heights High School.

Independence High School.

Madison High School.

Antigo High School.

University of California-Los Angeles.

Jeremiah Burke High School.

Alpine High School.

Townville Elementary School.

Vigor High School.

Linden McKinley STEM Academy.

June Jordan High School for Equity.

Union Middle School.

Mueller Park Junior High School.

West Liberty-Salem High School.

University of Washington.

King City High School.

North Park Elementary School.

North Lake College.

Freeman High School.

Mattoon High School.

Rancho Tehama Elementary School.

Aztec High School.

Wake Forest University.

Italy High School.

NET Charter High School.

Marshall County High School.

Sal Castro Middle School.

Marjory Stoneman Douglas High School

Great Mills High School

Central Michigan University

Huffman High School

Frederick Douglass High School

Forest High School

Highland High School

Dixon High School

Santa Fe High School

Noblesville West Middle School

University of North Carolina Charlotte

STEM School Highlands Ranch

Edgewood High School

Palm Beach Central High School

Providence Career & Technical Academy

Fairley High School (school bus)

Canyon Springs High School

Dennis Intermediate School

Florida International University

Central Elementary School

Cascade Middle School

Davidson High School

Prairie View A & M University

Altascocita High School

Central Academy of Excellence

Cleveland High School

Robert E. Lee High School

Cheyenne South High School

Grambling State University

Blountsville Elementary School

Holmes County, Mississippi (school bus)

Prescott High School

College of the Mainland

Wynbrooke Elementary School

UNC Charlotte

Riverview Florida (school bus)

Second Chance High School

Carman-Ainsworth High School

Williwaw Elementary School

Monroe Clark Middle School

Central Catholic High School

Jeanette High School

Eastern Hills High School

DeAnza High School

Ridgway High School

Roginald F. Lewis High School

Saugus High School

Pleasantville High School

Waukesha South High School

Oshkosh High School

Catholic Academy of New Haven

Bellaire High School

North Crowley High School

McAuliffe Elementary School

South Oak Cliff High School

Texas A&M University-Commerce

Sonora High School

Western Illinois University

Oxford High School

Robb Elementary

There are things we can do to make a difference today.

We believe that children are acting out in such ways for a greater purpose. They have a message to tell and it's about time that we listen, don't you think?

Yes, our youth is desperately crying out for help. It begins between the ages of one and two. If the temper tantrums get out of control and continue into grade school, then oppositional defiant disorder will more likely develop.

The term "terrible twos" was coined in the early 1950s, right around the time society began "competing with the Jones" and when corporal punishment turned into time-outs. Coincidence?

No, we are not, at all, saying that we should go back to spanking our children. We're saying that there is:
- a way to guide our children with empowerment and love...
- a way that motivates them to choose to engage in their lives without having to control their behavior at all...
- a way where you get everything you want as a parent, and they get what they want and need as children or teenagers.

The truth is that "terrible twos" is truly nothing more than a spirit that is not being heard or recognized. It is evidence that your child's victim side is growing stronger.

"Terrible twos" is not a normal part of childhood; it has simply become normal because that is how a human responds to being controlled. Doesn't that make so much sense?

I know you're working to keep them safe, but what is your actual role as a parent? Can you put it in words? What is your responsibility? Do you constantly nag your child, follow them around and tell them what to do? Or, do you acknowledge their desire and show them what to do to make their desire happen?

It's time we start looking in the right places for definite solutions... yes? Can we agree that guns are not the problem? Guns don't shoot people; people shoot people. And these are unhappy people with no vision, purpose or direction.

It is up to you to help your children live a life of purpose, on purpose.

CHAPTER 3

Potential of a Child

"Children are better off guided in advance rather than punished as a reaction." — Dr. John Locke

It's easy to see that — although no one desires this — our culture has created a generation of youths who are entitled, ungrateful blamers that cry when things don't go their way.

To make a difference for our children, studying history is imperative. It will help us understand our past and our present. This is part of your parenting foundation! People often say that "history repeats itself." Yes, the successes and failures of the past will help us narrow down what works. It can also help us avoid repeating horrific mistakes that do not work.

Let's begin with one of our favorite famous philosophers from the 17th century, Dr. John Locke. Until he labelled the job of parents "parenting," the term did not exist. Locke expressed that children are born without any inherent idea of how the world works.

Children are born without knowing:
- what manners are;
- how to tie their shoes;
- how to drive a car;
- what respect looks like; and
- the proper way to sit on a chair to eat dinner.

Children are born without knowing anything!

Locke pointed out that children are born with a perfect blank slate. A baby's mind is open and ready for whatever their parents are willing to help them develop. This does not mean that children are born without a specific personality or that they're not individuals because, of course, they are. We've already discussed this!

What Locke recognized was that children are born with pure potential.

With open minds. Zero habits. None bad. None good. Locke shared how children are better guided in advance rather than punished as a reaction.
Still, for hundreds of years, society domesticated their youth by placing fear into children's hearts.

Before the mid-1920s, the "parenting industry" did not even exist. No one brought their children to a doctor for behavior issues like they do today.

What Was the Difference?

- Purpose — Parents had more children so they would have more help on the farm. If a child wanted to eat, they were expected to contribute, to work and be part of their tribe or community.
- Life Skills — Because the purpose for more children was more help on the farm, it was essential to spend time with them so the parent's efforts could be duplicated.

- Earned Privileges — Wealth was having an excellent crop to sell in the summer. If a child wanted to do something or own something like a fishing pole, he earned it!

- Corporal Punishment — When a child did something a parent or teacher didn't like, the child would be beaten with a switch or locked in a closet as a form of punishment.

The concept back then was very much "Do as I say, or else!" This is what you call authoritarian parenting.

Authoritarian Parenting:

Strict rules, corporal punishment, children were to be seen and not heard.

In the 1920s, teenagers as young as 13 were considered adults. They were off building their own houses, getting married and having babies. There was no blaming. It was "If it is to be, it's up to me!" "If I want to have a house, I will have to build it." That's how the world was, and still is or should be. I mean, who's going to prepare meals, do laundry and clean your child's house after they move out?

John Watson, a child psychologist from the 1920s, shared in his popular child-rearing book, Psychological Care of the Infant and Child, that a good parent should not kiss and cuddle their babies. This was the moment mothers began to doubt their motherly instincts.

Entering the "competing with the Jones'" era, the focus of moms became more on the scientific studies of parenthood rather than duplicating life skills. Parents were taught to put their babies on a strict feeding and sleeping schedule. If you wavered off that schedule, you were considered a bad parent. Watson also mentioned that babies who were catered to would become wussy adults.

Everything changed in 1946 when Dr. Benjamin Spock published a book called Baby and Child Care. The book became a national phenomenon, selling more copies than any other non-fiction book for 52 years in a row (with the exception of the King James Bible).

For the first time in the history of the world, Spock taught parents the complete opposite from anything taught before. His position was that parents should cater to their children's every whim. Then, when the child does something naughty, use a naughty time or, as Supernanny calls it, "the naughty mat."

But, how does sitting your child on the stairs for a few minutes teach them what to do to make what's important to them show up?

Parents were taught that their children require a massive amount of attention to thrive. Beyond this awareness, they were left to fill in the missing pieces of this imperative life role called parenting!

JFK once quoted: "Children are only as good as what they have been taught." Aren't you and I just big kids who are only as good as what we've been taught? Being raised with an authoritarian parenting style left most of our parents lost and living in a world that no longer existed.

"Spock says don't spank! I don't know what to do to get you to listen to me!" is a statement I recall hearing from my mother. Yelling and nagging became the only known way to scare a child into complying with adult requests. This was the beginning of authoritative parenting — think Supernanny — and the onset of child mental health disorders.

<u>Authoritative Parenting:</u> Authoritative parents are responsive to the child's emotional needs while having high standards. They set limits and are very consistent in enforcing boundaries.

This sounds pretty good to loving and caring moms and dads. However, I'm sure you will agree that *something is wrong here*. Not only are our children showing signs of mental disorders more than ever before, they are speaking out in the only way they know how — meltdowns, anxiety, depression, disrespect, bullying, school gun shootings, and lastly but not least...suicide.

Speaking of suicide, I find it quite disturbing that on December 24th, 1983, Spock's grandson would shock the world - 37 years after Baby and Childcare was published. At 22, Peter Spock was found dead in the Boston's Children Museum parking lot, where his father, Michael Spock, worked as a director.

Do you think it's a coincidence that Spock's grandson committed suicide, and today suicide is the number one cause of teenage death on a global scale — following Spock's lead?

Action Step: Decide right now that you're going to read this entire book!

Take a recipe or cue card and write on it: "I will complete the entire Raising Healthy, Happy, Cooperative Kids book, so I can have a strong parenting foundation to build on for the sake of my children's lives."

CHAPTER 4

ADHD~21st Century Pandemic Child Disorder

*The DSM did not recognize
ADHD in the first edition at all!*

Pandemic: (of a disease) prevalent throughout an entire country, continent, or world; epidemic over a large area.

The entire globe is currently being overloaded with information about ADHD. The overwhelming evidence that this disorder will cause a lifelong struggle with focus has made us all susceptible to the biggest lie in the history of humanity.

I'm sure that almost every time you log on to your computer or watch television, you hear the word ADHD in some form or fashion. There's more attention on ADHD, ODD, autism, Asperger's, anxiety and depression than ever before! But, who knows the best solution? If you ask three people to define ADHD, you are sure to get three different answers.

In an attempt to help parents find solutions, ADHD and ODD are regularly discussed on television...acted out in movies...talked about in documentaries. ADHD, ODD, autism, anxiety and depression have become household names. And this is not okay!

Medical Description of ADHD:
Attention deficit hyperactivity disorder (ADHD)
- affects children and teens and can continue into adulthood. ADHD is the most commonly diagnosed mental disorder of children. Children with ADHD may be hyperactive and unable to control their impulses. Or they may have trouble paying attention. These behaviors interfere with school and home life.
- It's more common in boys than in girls. It's usually discovered when a child begins to have problems paying attention during the early school years.
- Adults with ADHD may have trouble managing time, organizing, setting goals, and holding down a job. They may also have problems with relationships, self-esteem and addiction.

Symptoms in Children are Grouped into Three Categories:

Inattention. A child with ADHD:
- is easily distracted;
- doesn't follow directions or finish tasks;
- doesn't appear to be listening;
- doesn't pay attention and makes careless mistakes;
- forgets about daily activities;
- has problems organizing daily tasks;
- doesn't like to do things that require sitting still;
- often loses things; and
- tends to daydream.

Hyperactivity. A child with ADHD:
- often squirms, fidgets, or bounces when sitting;
- doesn't stay seated;
- has trouble playing quietly;
- is constantly moving, such as running or climbing on things (In teens and adults, this is more commonly described as restlessness);
- talks excessively; and
- is always "on the go" as if "driven by a motor."

Impulsivity. A child with ADHD:
- has trouble waiting for their turn;
- blurts out answers; and
- interrupts others.

Later, we will show you exactly how each of these habits is developed. For now, let's just put all the medical terms for the most common childhood behavior disorders in one area.

Oppositional Defiant Disorder:
If your child or teenager has a frequent and persistent pattern of anger, irritability, arguing, defiance or vindictiveness toward you and other authority figures, they may have oppositional defiant disorder (ODD).

Asperger's syndrome:
A developmental disorder characterized by significant difficulties in social interaction and nonverbal communication, along with restricted and repetitive patterns of behavior and interests.

Autism:
Difficulty in communicating and forming relationships with other people and in using language and abstract concepts.

We get that, yes, these symptoms exist. Of course, they do. Children are born without any developed life skills.

Zip.
Zero.
None.

Everything we wish for them to know and do, we must teach them. You may want to read the preceding sentence repeatedly until you get it… until you see it. If you want your child to know how to sit up straight on a chair, you must show them exactly what you think sitting up straight on a chair looks like.

The *Diagnostic and Statistical Manual of Mental Disorders* (DSM), which as first released in 1952, listed all recognized mental disorders. It also included known causes, risk factors, and suggested treatments for each condition. The DSM is updated for doctors to study regularly and is still used as a reference today.

This is interesting: The American Psychology Association (APA) did not recognize ADHD in the first edition at all! None of the childhood behavior disorders existed in the medical books!

The second edition of DSM was later published in 1968. With the help of Dr. Leon Eisenberg, this edition included hyperkinetic impulse disorder for the first time. This was renamed to attention deficit disorder (ADD) and renamed again to attention deficit hyperactive disorder (ADHD) — just in the last decade or so.

Eisenberg received the Ruane Prize for Child and Adolescent Psychiatry Research. For more than 40 years, he was a known leader in child psychiatry through his work with pharmacological trials, research, teaching, social policy, and his **theories of autism and social medicine**.

Read that again!

It's very telling that they call his life's work "theories." In one article, Eisenberg mentions that so many parents were bringing their children to the doctor's office for disruptive behavior that they created a name and developed a medication as a simple and easy fix.

"ADHD is a prime example of a fictitious disease," were the words of Dr. Leon Eisenberg, the same "scientific father of ADHD" mentioned above. He said this during his final interview before his death at age 87 in 2009.

Nearly a decade after his deathbed confession, more than a million toddlers as young as one and two are now being diagnosed with ADHD and prescribed a psycho-stimulant medication. Well-meaning parents who cannot control their youngster's crying believe something is wrong with them. They bring their toddlers to the doctor's office in droves to request medication without proactive parenting tools.

Here's the kicker... there are no scientific tests to validate any child behavior disorder.

Nada.
Zilch.

Here's how it works:

1. A child is sent to school without practicing sitting still in a chair and with zero motivation to engage.
2. Say the child does not sit still or pay attention in class.
3. Their parent receives an invitation to discuss their child's disruptive behavior.
4. The parent fills in a simple questionnaire provided by the school counsellor.
5. The pediatrician writes a prescription that will calm the child down.
6. The child calms down.

Talk about immediate gratification! Yes, you can create rapid change with medication. Yes, the teacher's life may be more manageable. Yes, the parents' lives may be more manageable. BUT, what is the child learning? If you can find some way to convince us that this solution will genuinely elevate a child to succeed in this world, please send us an email immediately!

Do you believe:
- medicating children is teaching them how to learn life skills; and
- medicating children will teach them that medication is the solution to all their emotional problems?

Medicating children does not drive them to develop the habit of focus, nor does it show the child how to sit still on a chair or pay attention.

It takes 100 years for an oak tree to mature, while a squash grows in two months. Why are we in such a hurry to calm our kids? It takes 18 years for a child to develop, not six. We are treating our children like squashes when we should be treating them more like oak trees.

Can you get it back tomorrow if you waste all your time today? Nope. Whatever you don't use, you lose.
Imagine if you tied your arm to your chest and left it like that for three months...would you lose the use of your arm? You bet! At least for a while.

Your children would love to please you. They have a desire to feel important. Every child deserves the same opportunity to develop focus and self-control. What makes these life skills any different than the opportunity to learn how to walk? Just as a bodybuilder must maintain their muscles with consistent weight lifting, a child will only learn new thought patterns with constant practice.

Can you see that every single symptom listed in childhood behavior and mental disorders can be developed with sustained regular use and conscious effort? Go back and look at the list of symptoms. Is there anything that your child can't learn?

I once had a mentor tell me: "Awareness is the key to greatness." First, you become aware. Then, you can learn a new skill through consistent repetition and become great! Otherwise, we can spend our entire lives in ignorance — unconsciously incompetent.

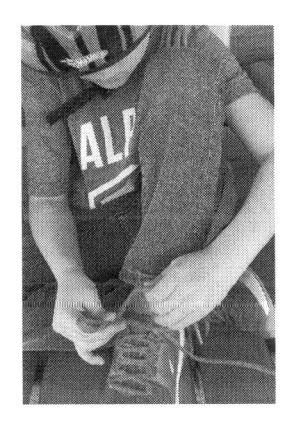

A child who can learn to tie their shoes or play a video game can learn to wait their turn — if their hunger for the result was strong enough. If a child seems to be constantly angry, he needs to learn to organize his thoughts and master emotions. If a child doesn't know how to find happiness, he simply cannot see it on his own. If he could, he would.

Remember, at the beginning of this book, we shared that a prerequisite for making authentic change is the ability to hope? Ask yourself this question... how many of the listed child behavior disorder symptoms affecting your child have you taken the time to teach him authentically?

After asking hundreds of parents this question, a funny thing happened. We noticed the same answer over and over and over again. The only logical conclusion is that child mental disorders become real when we, as parents, accept them...when we miss the natural transition from feeding our kids fish to teaching them to become independent fishermen.

CHAPTER 5

Your Role

"There's no way to be logical with an angry adult, let alone an angry child."

Can you put your role or job description as a parent in writing?

Is it to:
- protect your children;
- make them happy;
- lavish them with attention;
- make them feel loved; or
- all of the above?

I'm positive that you would choose to protect your children from harm, lavish them with attention, and keep them happy. But, is that your role in your children's lives?

Let's look to nature for a moment...
Imagine if all the bunny rabbits in the world suddenly decided to lavish their offspring with attention, protect them from predators, and go out of their way to make their young happy. What would happen to the baby bunnies once they became adults and their parents were sick of tending to their every need? Would they have the skills to survive on their own? We all know that the answer is a big fat "NO!"

From whales to bears, there are imperative life skills that must be passed down from generation to generation. In the beginning, your child is 100% dependent on you. Over time — we're sure you'll agree that it's your job to pass down important life skills so your child can feed and clothe themselves in the near future, right?

The one thing missing in nearly every parenting book and article we have found is that they do not say that our role for our children is to prepare them for life. The only one that comes close to explaining the importance of teaching our children how to master their emotions is in Dr. Leonard Sax's book, *The Collapse of Parenting*.

If a child could do things on their own, they would. Your children don't wake up wondering the best way to make you upset in the morning.

Look, you don't owe your children cable television, wifi and cell phones. You owe your children life skills, including morals and virtues like responsibility, respect, focus and self-control. You know this intuitively, yes?.

We teach our babies to:
- hold a fork;
- walk when the time is right;
- get up and keep trying even though they continue to fall down;
- go to the bathroom on their own; and
- get a glass of water themselves — hopefully.

If your child wants something to drink, they can get it independently. And if not, it Is up to you to teach them how, and allow some struggle.

You can easily find parenting experts offering parenting tips like "Get down on your child's level and speak in an authoritative voice." But is this going to help your child learn to get what's important to them in a solution-oriented and proactive way without you there?

Focusing on solutions for temper tantrums, meltdowns and angry outbursts is a backward way of thinking. It places the child as the cause and the parent's reaction as the effect. This also puts the child in a leadership position. It matches nature's law of cause and effect in a highly frustrating way for all.

We speak with new parents every day who share that they are desperate for answers dealing with a defiant child. The natural habit is always "What do I do when my child does this?" Can you see that this is a reactive way of thinking? It's like jumping out of an airplane without a parachute and then asking, "What do I do now?"

Psychology Today says that emotions override rational thought. There's no way to be logical with an angry adult, let alone an angry child.

This is a perfect scientific equation for negative results like:

- anger;
- anxiety;
- depression;
- chaos;
- broken relationships;
- misunderstandings;
- miscommunication; and
- a hundred other negative emotions and circumstances.

If this is what you're after, following your current parenting style has you right on track. Can you see the truth about this?

Here's the formula for a toxic home or class environment:

Child's Ignorant Action + Parent's Angry Reaction = **Stress**

Most of society is focused on today's poor child behavior from an adult perspective. We are not taking the time to teach them their expectations in advance.

Dr. Leonard Sax shares an on-point passage in his book, *The Collapse of Parenting,* "When his parents didn't buy him the toy he wanted, he would scream in the toy store. But his parents had never taught him the rules of good behavior. His behavior was pretty much what you would expect of a kid who has never known consistent discipline."

He confirmed that the boy has a habit of crying in the store because it's worked for him in the past. Instead of consistent discipline, however, we would look at consistent practice showing him how to get a toy when he goes to the store.

We tend to know this in our business lives or at our jobs. Can you imagine showing up for your first day of work not knowing what to do at all? Everyone assumes you do, but every time you go to make a move, they yell at you.

> "No, we don't do that!"
> "Stop it!"
> "Shut up!"
> "Don't touch!"

Would you now know what to do? How long would you be happy and choose to work in that environment? What if you were stuck there? You have no choice but to live in this dictational and unproductive, hellish environment. How happy could you possibly feel? You're right! You couldn't feel happiness at all.

Here, let me draw it out for you again.

Worker's Action + Boss's Reaction =
Frustration

Here's an example of **reactive parenting:**

It's a beautiful afternoon. You don't want to be cooped up on such a lovely day with screaming kids who constantly bug each other. You decide it would be fun to take your small children for a walk to the park. You excitedly announce the idea to your children and walk over to turn the television off.

"Okay, let's get our jacket and shoes on so we can go for a walk to the park," you dictate, cheerfully. You finally get to enjoy some fun with your little love bunnies! But your cheerful demeanor begins to dissipate as confusion and anxiety set in.

On the flip side, your children don't seem as excited about going for a walk as you are. They are upset that you turned the television off. And in an attempt to avoid a power struggle, you successfully distract them. You turn their attention to the great outdoors.

Phew … meltdown averted! Yay!

You gather your little ones up and head out the door to the park… hoping your outing is fun and worth the effort. Before you know it, they're happily running up and down the sidewalk.

But, you have been here before, or you've heard a story, and you begin to feel worried. The fear you are feeling begins to cause a panic alarm inside your mind. As annoyed as you are with your toddlers, you love your children immensely. You want them to be safe. So, you begin to yell, "Hey, little Sally, come back to Mommy!"

Now your younger child, who's two, thinks you are playing a game. She begins to run further away. Your worst nightmare is happening!

You yell louder. As your panic heightens, she seems to be running faster and faster directly toward the busy street ahead. You throw everything to the ground in a mad rush! All you can think about is catching her before she gets to the main road and is hit by a car!

Your toddler is giggling. She appears to be laughing at you, which causes you to become angry. You don't want to experience this again. Ever! Never!

You reach her just as she approaches the street.

You yell at her.
You spank her!

You make her feel bad to relate the bad feeling to the experience. You believe you are teaching her in order to protect her, right? All the while, your toddler knows nothing of the danger on the streets. From her point of view, she was simply playing with you. She trusted you to show her the ropes and be on her side.

In an attempt to protect your baby from danger, you unknowingly wound her soul. It's a wound you can't see, but it's there. It's a wound that will affect her subconscious thoughts forever.

Does this scenario sound familiar to you? It's like parenting today is in constant reaction to poor child behavior. It's causing most moms to live in a continuous state of stress and frustration with their children.

Maybe your child doesn't run on the streets. Perhaps he yells or runs in the house. What's your go-to statement for when your children do something you don't like? Do the words and actions you use show your children exactly what you want them to do to please you?

With all that being said, if you begin lecturing your child on the way the world works, will he get what you're saying? Can he fast forward his mind and know what it's like to be an adult?

If you have a **goal** to raise healthy, happy, cooperative kids, all you need to do is become the cause in the universal truth of cause and effect.

You can create a proactive plan for your child and teach them what to do in advance!

Antoine de Saint-Exupéry, a famous 1930s children's book author and philosopher, said,
"A goal without a plan is just a wish or a dream."

In the 16th century, Benjamin Franklin wrote,
"By failing to prepare, you are preparing to fail."

The Bible tells us that people without a vision perish.
Proverbs 29:18 Where there is no vision, the people perish: but he that keepeth the law, happy is he.

We plan our weddings, vacations and home renovations. We do not design our lives with our children. We don't lay out our children's life skills and then plan to achieve what we desire. We should.

We are winging it with the ones we love most in the world, our babies. We demand respect. We dictate and control every aspect of their lives and then wonder what's wrong with them. Right now, you are reacting to and cleaning up after your kids most of every day in a chaotic, exhausting and frustrating environment, right?

To learn anything, we must first see what it should look like. Then, we need a good learning environment to experience it independently. This is the only way to learn. We must have experienced the failure, emotion or success to choose and engage in free will.

Seeing creates awareness. Doing a thing over and over again makes a life skill. Let's say you want your children to put their toys away. Yelling at them, "Put your toys away," is dictation and is a habit that is not serving you. To teach a life skill, you must show your child what something looks like, mess it all back up, and then have them show you what that something looks like — until they can do it as well as you do.

Show your children - don't tell them!

CHAPTER 6

The Goal

When you have a family plan in place, There'll be no questions like "What do I do when my child does this?"

Look, the truth is that you have been domesticated, trained and conditioned to believe that to be a good parent means you do everything for your children. Thank you, Dr. Spock!
Ironically, look at the results of his grandson... not good, right?

Are you with us on this?

If you let your child make their lunch, and someone calls you a bad parent, then so what? Who cares about what they think?

If you:
- don't teach your child how to feed themselves now, how are they ever going to survive if something happens to you?

- don't teach your child that they're good enough to make lunch on their own, how are they ever going to believe they can live a whole life without you?

- want order, peace and laughter, doesn't it make sense that you should do the opposite of the perfect scientific equation for bad feelings?

Let's take a look at what creates more love and joy:

> Parent's Plan + Child's Practiced Action =
> ## Harmony

The above formula means that if you have a goal and your child has a goal, all you have to do is proactively develop a plan which both of you can focus on.

On the one hand, it is your job to create a plan for your child to follow and teach the matching life skills. Have you ever played Simon Says? That's a beautiful example of a game you can play with your child that will teach self-control, focus and following directions.

On the other hand, your child's job is to learn said life skills by following what you teach them. Can you see how important it is to develop a plan and give proactive attention to your children?

When you have a family plan in place, there will be no questions like "What do I do when my child does this?" You would simply look at your child's weekly Star Chart and see the results. No, not a chore chart, or a boundary chart, a Star Chart. A chart focussed all on the child's goals and productivity.

If little Timmy decides to have a temper tantrum, your proactive plan for what happens next should be crystal clear for both you and your child — before anger sets in. When little Timmy chooses to have a temper tantrum, little Timmy decides to hang out in his room for a few minutes. If he chooses to use his words, he unlocks the privilege of watching television, playing games or another privilege your child is working towards. This is not a punishment given as a reaction to the behavior you don't like. It's a proactive and agreed-upon plan based on the actions he chooses — AFTER YOU TAKE THE TIME TO TEACH THEM.

Decide everything upfront. Then take the time to show your children exactly what actions get crystal clear results. Your child's entire learning environment will transform from reactive to proactive when you do this. You'll have a vision. You'll be more confident, and so will your child.

Think about it like this... when your child is upset about something, he's coming to you as a customer service department. You are the person in charge. To add, they don't have the skills or vocabulary to tell you, "Hey, Mom! I need life skills here." They will tell you in the only way they know how: they would throw temper tantrums and get depressed or angry. They would whine. They would cry. They would hit.

Because of constant dictation and control, your children are just figuring things out independently. Since whining has worked for them in the past, they will continue to escalate the same known life skill throughout childhood. If not evaluated, this pattern will lead to that child eventually becoming diagnosed with a behavior or emotional disorder and prescribed medication.

Going back to the customer support analogy... If you went to a customer service department to complain because a product you bought didn't work and you didn't know how to fix it, how would you like them to respond?

What if they responded with "I'm sorry, I don't do that"? Wouldn't you be angry?

"Listen, you are not hearing me! You're deaf, so I'm going to yell louder," will be more likely your response out of frustration.

Maybe your child has never learned the simple game of opposites. They won't know they can turn obstacles into opportunities unless you teach them that. Maybe your child has never learned to negotiate or been shown what respect looks like. Demanding your child to respect you does not show them what it looks like.
If you change the root cause, you must change the effect, yes? Choose what life skills your children need to learn, and then teach them until they can duplicate you!

Action Plan:

Create a master list of life skills you still need to teach your child before becoming an adult. As soon as your list is in writing, it becomes a goal.

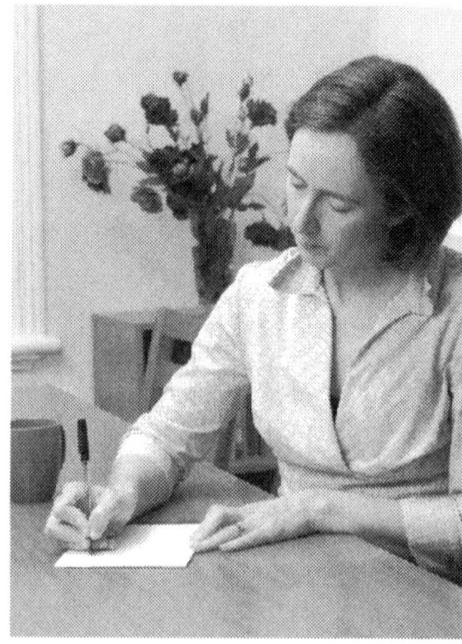

CHAPTER 7

Win-Win Plan

More opportunity to be independent is the cure for the lack of confidence we see in today's children.

Children love showing off their greatness. You can identify this by how often your child shouts, "Look what I did, Mom!"

The opportunity to be independent is the cure for the lack of confidence we see in many of today's children. After all, if a parent does for the child what he should be doing on his own, the message is clear: "You don't think I have what it takes to do it on my own."

It's okay if they fail.
Allow your children to fail.

Encourage your child to persevere through obstacles, and help them develop neural pathways that will set them up for a massive amount of success later in life.

Many parents share that their baby was happy until they were around 18 months old. So, what changes our beautiful, happy babies into terrible twos or horrific threes? At around 18 months old, babies begin to get into everything. Their curious nature is what gives them a zest for life. Toddlers begin to desire more opportunities to explore. "Mommy, look what I did!" But, to Mom and Dad, the baby becomes a pain in the royal butt!

Hey! I get it. I was a mom of four children who were under the age of six at the same time. I thought I was a superhero. I did everything for them. I was there for them. I read them stories every night. They had the best clothes, individual rooms, and every toy and gadget you could think of. Still, they were unruly, ungrateful, and disrespectful. What I was doing wasn't working!

I was following Supernanny, using timeouts and takeaways. I had no idea why my children were so angry. In fact, like the majority of us, I believed that angry toddlers were typical. Now I see a toddler who wishes to do something as an opportunity to teach, not punish.

Imagine your toddler or child saying something, sharing something, or showing interest in something. Wouldn't it be awful to tell him no, can't do, or that won't work?

Here are a few examples for different ages:

Toddler:
Bang on a glass table.

Preschooler:
Asks for a cookie 20 minutes before dinner.

Young Child:
Draws on the couch with a crayon.

Teenager:
She wants to get her belly button pierced.

It doesn't matter how old your child is, you must realize that at each level of development, your child will desire something that you won't like.

Let's take the toddler example:

Your three-year-old states, "I want a cookie."

"Not right now, little guy. Supper's in twenty minutes," you respond as nicely and as calmly as possible.

"Awe... but I want a cookie!" Your toddler begins to whine as you brace yourself for a complete meltdown.

"I said no! If you keep whining, I'm going to put you in a timeout," you say.

Can you see how this scenario will result in more whining? We have already shared the perfect scientific equation for chaos, frustration, anger and desperation — overall negative energy.

Now, you're right if you think your job is to help your child create good habits. We know that eating cookies right before dinner is not a great one.

Can you at least validate his desire for a cookie and tell him that it's normal to love cookies?

Can you ask him what he loves about cookies and which one is his favorite?

Looking back, I now know I couldn't see my child's pain. I'm still heartbroken about it. It was so innocent. I just wanted them to be happy and know how loved they were.

Are you open to looking at your children through an **educational lens vs. a behavioral lens** moving forward? If you are, validation is empowering and the first new habit to create. Begin to recognize what's important to them. This action alone will pay off huge dividends both now and later in life! Validating everything they ask for, without judgement, will bring you and your child more confidence and feelings of worthiness.

You only know what you know. What you know has been passed down to you unconsciously from the people who loved you the most, your parents. What result are you looking for as a parent?

Would you like to be a more empowering parent than yours were? If you do, then you must do something different. Right?

I once heard a story about a woman who brought home a ham for Christmas dinner. Before she placed it in the pot to cook it, she cut both ends off. Her daughter was watching and asked, "Mom, why do you cut the ends off the ham?"

Mom paused a moment and then answered, "I don't know, that's just what I've always done. I saw my Mom doing that when I was a little girl".

When Grandma arrived for Christmas dinner, the question was brought up: "Grandma – why did you cut the ends off the ham before placing it in the oven?"

"I don't know," Grandma replied. "Your great-grandma used to do that – so it's just something I've always done!"

Later, the family travelled to great-grandma's house to share Christmas tea. During a lull in the conversation, the granddaughter asked,

"Nana, why do you cut the end off the ham before cooking it?"

"Well," replied the Great-Grandmother, "When your grandma was a young girl, my oven was tiny. I couldn't fit the whole ham in without cutting the ends off."

Now, I don't know if this is a real story or not, but — why would we continue to do what we already know doesn't work just because that's what our parents did? It's because that's all we know to do unless we begin to educate ourselves — on purpose!

It's time to think for ourselves and to step up for the sake of our children, don't you think? Taking the time to acknowledge what your child is interested in vs. automatically telling them no is life-changing in itself.

Do you want to follow the equation that will guarantee you joy-filled days of laughter with your kids? All you need to do is plan to achieve your parenting goals and attach them to your child's goals.

> (PG + CG) + Parent Plan + Child Action =
> ## Desired Effect

Here's how it works:

1. You have a goal to enjoy a family dinner.
2. Your child has a goal for a cookie.
3. You validate what's important to them.
4. Share your parent-approved plan with your child.
5. Teach them to do precisely what you want through role play.
6. Give them something to work for - the cookie!

I'm sure you can see how this will create a win-win plan vs. a win-lose plan. You know, where you win, and they lose? "Why won't they just listen to me?" And, you kind of lose too, don't you?

Here's a better way to communicate your desire:

"I'd love for you to have a cookie. Did you want half a cookie, a whole cookie or two cookies?"

Your child would respond, "Ummm…I want two cookies."

You can then say, "Perfect! When you sit at the table like this."

After this, SHOW him exactly what that looks like. Have him mimic what you're doing so he can show you he knows what you mean.

"And you eat SOME of your dinner, you'll make HALF a cookie show up".

"You can make ONE cookie show up if you eat ALL your dinner BUT get up from the dinner table."

"But, if you sit at the table like this AND you eat ALL your dinner, you can make TWO cookies show up."

Perfecting the skill of pre-framing takes a little or, in some cases, much practice. Most of us have been dictating and punishing for several years already. Those parenting skills are deeply ingrained and habitual.

At first, making the change from chaos to order will feel like it did when you first learned to tie your shoes or drive a car. It's going to feel uncomfortable. It will be worth it!

Consciously learning to become a proactive parent rather than a reactive one will mean you get to be your child's hero. In a loving, guiding and empowering way, you can pass on all of the life skills and characteristics you choose for them to know!

You won't have to be the bearer of bad news. You won't have to be your child's opponent by telling him "NO". You won't need to yell at your child ever again. Ever!

You'll know exactly how to motivate your children to work toward goals they choose for themselves.

The only known way to help a child be happy is to help them build confidence. A child builds confidence by persevering through struggle while working toward important things, i.e. goals.

Here's an example: Scenario #1 (The "old" you)

Let's say your child asks for a $500 bike; they don't understand money yet. Even teenagers don't know money unless they've ever had to earn it.
Let's say that this child is between eight and 12. They don't understand you had to put in 14 hours of

overtime to earn enough money for a new couch. There's no way to understand that concept until they experience it.

"Hi, Mom! I'm so excited! I saw this bike. It's so awesome! All the cool kids have one."

You would probably go into rescue mode and feel responsible. Right?

What if you just bought him a bike? "Ummm, I just bought you a great bike. It can wait."

Can you see the look of devastation on your child's face? What feeling matches that outcome? Is it a good or bad feeling?

They hear "no" to what's important to them. They feel unworthy. They feel hopeless. If you don't make it happen, there must be no way to get what he really wants. You're his hero, after all. You're his way to making things happen until you teach him otherwise.

How depressing is that? "The other kids are better than me." "I'm not good enough." No matter how you look at it, your child will feel bad. Say it with a sweet voice. Be as nice as you can be. It still won't help your child understand. They can't. They shouldn't.

Imagine this: Scenario #2 (The "new" you)

"Wow! I would love for you to have that bike! What color do you want your bike to be?"

Simple <u>validation</u> will <u>empower</u> him. It will show him that what's important to him is essential to you too.

"Did you see a bike?"

"Who do you know who has that bike?"

"What is it about that bike that you like?"

Asking questions will let your child have a chance to share what's important to him. Take thirty seconds to five minutes to hear him out. If he does want to earn that bike, share some money-making ideas with him. Perhaps asking him, "What are you willing to trade?"

"I'm going to make flyers and help people mow their lawns for money! I'm going to make it happen!" This can be the response when they realize they are in control of their desire showing up.

We have no idea what picture our children hold in their minds. Your child may simply want to share something exciting with you. It's entirely possible that he doesn't really want what he's asked for badly enough to earn it himself.

Encouraging him either way will take the pressure off you being the only option for him to reach his goals. Teaching him to earn his privileges will prepare him for the real world.

This is how you teach children:

- responsibility
- work ethic
- gratitude
- delayed gratification
- persistence
- independence
- desire
- purpose
- AND so much more!

It's the ONLY way!

I mean, who are we to:

- tell a child with desire, "NO"?
- OR give them what they want and kill their passion?

When you understand this valuable truth, you will see your child's genius. Seeing your children through an education lens will give power to the next generation.
If you find your child upset or angry, simply take a moment and ask a few questions.

- Do you want me to help you?
- What are you having trouble with?
- What's another way you can think of?
- What is it you're angry about?
- What are you looking to do that isn't working yet?
- Do you need some alone time?

If you feel bad for your child and take over, he won't feel empowered. He'll feel unworthy.

Working toward a personal goal creates excitement and enthusiasm. It is the only variable that gives our lives, including our children, purpose.

Persevering through a struggle to accomplish a definite purpose will develop characteristics that will help your children thrive throughout life!

CHAPTER 8

Guiding Behavior

A child can only see the world from their own experiences.

It's imperative to understand that your children see the world entirely differently than you do. A child can only see the world from their own experiences while an adult brain has 20, 30, even 50 years of experience. These experiences create millions of neural pathways. The human brain comprises an estimated 100 billion neurons making 100 trillion neural connections.

A child who is left to make choices without a defined plan and practiced life skills will inevitably do something that does not please their parent. One of the main problems with communicating with children is that we believe they can think abstract. They can't.

Children cannot physically think abstract until they're at least the age of 13. This means that a child can bring you a cup but cannot explain what a cup is. When you ask your child questions like "What do you want to have for dinner tonight?" They're going to say the only thing they can think of like "Ice cream." "Kraft Dinner." "Pizza." "Hamburgers."

They will not say, "Mama, I'm five. Feed me nutrition. I'm growing, and I need to be healthy." So, you will need to create proactive plans by making parent-approved decisions and then offer a couple of choices.

When you catch a child drawing all over their bodies with a black marker, and you ask, "Why did you do that?" Their inability to think abstract will give you the only answer they can think of "I don't know."

This has <u>two meanings</u>:

1. "If I tell you about it, you'll yell at me."

2. "I have no idea how to explain the answer to you."

Your children cannot see your perspective. Your child's curious nature is their internal motivator. Your child lives life in daily wonder and awe. When you tell them no, can't, don't, stop, etc., their motivation weakens.

Here's an example:

You look at the couch and see a week or two's worth of work to have purchased it. They look at the sofa and see a trampoline. Do you see what we're saying?

If your child wishes to jump, show your child where she can jump and then allow her to choose a parent-approved goal to work toward. When it's something she determines that she wants, she'll be motivated to decide for herself the best place to jump consciously!

As we mentioned earlier, Dr. John Locke pointed out in the late 17th century that all children are born with no idea how the world works. If you don't teach your child life skills — sometimes over and over and over again until they get it — your child will miss specific imperative transformational windows.

It's your responsibility to equip your child with these skills so she can become an independent, solution-oriented thinker! Doesn't that just make so much sense?

You have 18 years to prepare your children for adulthood! You didn't give up on them when they were learning to walk. Take the time to teach them how to make their beds, clean their laundry, and make their food. Teach them how to sit still on a chair.

ROLEPLAY

PRACTICE

PERFECT

Make it your mission to teach them 1,000 life skills — necessary for a rich and successful life. Allow your children to struggle through obstacles. If they're turning the hose the wrong way, encourage them to figure out the right way on their own!

Protecting them too much denies them the opportunity to experience and learn. This is how you create dependence. Many of us are unknowingly doing just that!

> *"Children need models rather than critics."*
> *- Joseph Joubert*

Guiding Behavior:

Let's explore how to guide behavior with the same walk to the park story from earlier but executed in a more loving, guiding and empowering way:

It's a beautiful afternoon. You don't want to be cooped up on such a lovely day with screaming kids who constantly bug each other. Deciding it would be fun to take your small children for a walk to the park, you excitedly take a couple of minutes and think about what you want from your children.

"I want my children to walk by my side. I would love to see them keeping their hands to themselves and focused on being safe," you say.

Wondrous, that is called a goal. These are ideas that are important to you. What makes them essential to your children? What are they working toward?

You can ask your children this question. "Hey guys, would you like to go for a walk to the park now or when your show is over?"

Asking them a question with two already parent-approved decisions will transform the dynamic of your day.

"Ummm...when my show is over!"

"Awesome! Works for me."

When the show is over, you could ask them, "Would you like to go to the park for just a short time or a long time?"

"A long time!"

"Great! I would love to play at the park for a long time too. I'm happy to help you stay at the park until the big hand on the clock gets to 12. If you choose to walk beside me and focus on being safe from the big scary cars the entire way to the park, we can stay for a long time. If, however, you choose to run around or bug your brother, we'll go for just a short time."

And then have them repeat back the agreement. This is your plan to achieve both your goal and your child's goal. He will feel as if he has a say in his life. He gets to choose!

Oh, one more thing, when you pre-frame and role-play precisely what their part of the plan looks like before heading to the busy street, you'll create a brand new, fun and joyful experience. Your children will respond with, "Mom, I'll get right on it!"

Remember, one must experience what you're talking about before genuinely understanding what you're trying to say. When do you want to begin teaching your child life skills.

CHAPTER 9

Desire

A strong desire is what will push your child to persist through struggles and obstacles.

A child can only understand the world and his role in it in as much as he's lived it. Every experience is a new one. There is no worry, doubt, fear or even anger until he learns that, in some way, it works to get what's important to him.

- A newborn baby desires a clean diaper.
- A toddler desires a new toy or a snack.
- A child desires time outside or on video games or time with their friends.
- A teenager desires freedom.
- An adult desires vacations or to create memories.

We all have a desire for things. There's no question about that. We might not realize the importance of the emotion of desire and its power to create authentic harmony and peace in our homes with our children, but certainly, they are.

You have a desire for more quality time with your kids. You wish to experience an abundance of laughter and joy with them. Correct? Isn't that why you're taking the time to read this book right now?

If you were simply blessed with children who already knew how to make things happen in their lives, you'd have no desire to read this book. That is the truth.

We didn't give you that desire. Your desire was put there by the contrast you're currently experiencing with your children. Now, if you want a more peaceful, fun life with your children, you're forced to learn new skills. That's the power of contrast and what life's all about.

The point is that we grow and learn and become more through contrast. Imagine a baby is struggling to get up on a chair. If you decide to help that baby up, you are, at that moment, unknowingly stealing the feeling of accomplishment from that baby. You can believe you're trying to help your baby if you want to.

However, you will need to admit that in the end, it was that struggle that could have helped her develop her inner confidence and feeling of fulfillment, not to mention motor skills and muscle strength.

You see, we all desire purpose and the feeling of accomplishment. From the time we learn to crawl, tie our shoes or drive a car — it's the journey of transition that gives us meaning for life.

If your child is ten and he has a desire for a new bike, why not teach him how to earn that bike all on his own?

Why do we feel as if we're responsible for working for and then buying our children a new bike? Who are we to tell our child no if it's important to him?

"No. I just bought you a very expensive bike. How ungrateful. You can wait until next year." How does this line of thinking help a child learn he can work for his bike?

Desire is the first step toward the achievement of anything. A strong desire will push your child to persist through struggles and obstacles like studying for a test or taking the garbage out.

If you annihilate your child's desires by doing too much and giving them too much that they could not make things happen on their own, you annihilate their mind. How is that, you ask? If a child gets everything they desire handed to them on a silver platter, not only are they not learning gratitude and work ethic, they'll have zero fuel in their tank to take authority seriously.

Why should they:

- Learn to make money if you buy everything?
- Try in school if there's no child left behind?
- Listen to you instead of leaving the house when it doesn't affect their lives?

You see, when parents control every aspect of their child's life and then give them everything they desire, they're preparing their child perfectly for a world that does not exist. Is it any wonder why so many parents have trouble with their children's behavior?

CHAPTER 10

Creature of Habit

It is possible to form new neural pathways, developing new behavioral patterns through conscious repeated effort.

Research in human psychology tells us that human beings are creatures of habit. More than 95% of the actions we take daily are habitual. When you find yourself frustrated with your children, chances are you revert to subconscious or habitual behavior patterns like nagging, bribing or yelling. If you think about it, isn't most of your day — and also your child's day — operated by habitual behavior patterns? Reacting to your child's behavior without applying conscious choice will cause you to live in chaos.

A habitual behavior pattern is developed through routine behavior — repeated regularly. For example, you put your left or right foot in first when you put on pants or socks. Pay attention next time, and you'll see. If you try the other leg first, it'll feel uncomfortable.

New behavior patterns can become automatic through the process of new habit formation. To create lifelong authentic change, a strong desire must motivate people to persevere. This is why allowing your child to work toward a goal is a compelling strategy.

The American Journal of Psychology (1903) defines a habit from the standpoint of psychology as "a more or less fixed way of thinking, willing, or feeling acquired through previous repetition of a mental experience." Repeated human behavior patterns become imprinted in the brain by neural pathways. The American Journal of Psychology states that it is possible to form new neural pathways, developing new behavioral patterns through conscious repeated effort.

This practice of habit formation can be slow and difficult. Phillippa Lally is a health psychology researcher at the University College in London. In a study published in the European Journal of Social Psychology, Lally and her research team figured out how long it takes to form a habit.

The study examined the habits of 96 people over 12 weeks. In Lally's analysis, it took anywhere from 18 days to 254 days for people to form a new habit. A strong desire for a unique result will aid in developing a new, more healthy and effective routine.

3 Stages of a New Habit:

- **Cue:** This is the trigger that causes the behavior. Let's say your child cries in Toys R Us when you tell him no to getting a new toy. Telling your child no would be the cue.

- **Behavior:** What behavior comes to the surface when triggered with the cue? In this instance, crying is a habit. It could still be a habit from when he needed to be fed as a newborn.

- **Reward:** In developing all habits, there must be a goal, reward or positive feeling associated with the result. In the above example, the new toy at Toys R Us represents the reward.

If crying has ever worked to get the child what he wanted, the neural pathway to "Cry to get what I want" was developed. A new habit must replace the cry with a goal explicitly chosen by the child.

It's important to note that keystone habits are the gateway to developing new habits. So, if crying is a habit your child has developed as a way to get what he wants, this would be considered a keystone habit. If not changed, this will lead to other harmful habits like lying, cheating and stealing.

A great reward is only needed at the beginning of changing a habit. After repeating the desired behavior, the new pattern will prevail even without a reward. Once a neural pathway has been created, it must be consciously re-created.

Do you have a big goal and a big enough "why" to transform from being a reactive to proactive parent? Doing so will help your kids transform from defiant to cooperative. A conscious effort on your part will be required for an extended period.

Goals guide habits.

They provide a vision for a result that ignites motivation. Habits are often a trace of the pursuit of a past goal. An oppositional context occurs when a habit forces one action, but a conscious goal pushes for another one.

Anthony Dickinson and colleagues conducted a series of elegant experiments in the early 1980s at the University of Cambridge in England that exposed the behavioral differences between goal-directed and habitual processes. Basically, in the training phase, a rat was trained to press a lever to receive some food. Then, in a second phase, the rat was placed in a different cage without a lever and was given the food, but it was made ill whenever it ate the food. This caused the rat to "devalue" the food because it associated it with being sick without directly associating the action of pressing the lever with being ill.

Finally, the rat was placed in the original cage with the lever in the test phase. (To prevent additional learning, no food was delivered in the test phase.) Rats that underwent extensive training continued to press the lever in the test phase even though the food was devalued; their behavior was habitual. Rats that had undergone an intermediate training phase did not, and their behavior was called goal-directed.

CHAPTER 11

Parent Paradise

Your child needs you to step up and be their leader.

Can you think of a time when you believed something and then found out you were wrong? Remember the telephone game in elementary school? By the time your message went around the circle, it had changed.

Most of us believe that childhood labels like terrible twos, horrific threes or teenage rebellion are a normal part of life. Working with the idea that all children are born defiant, we've been missing the truth about their potential.

Some of us were introduced to ADHD when our children began school. If you're a younger generation under the age of 40, you learned about it while in school because you or one of your friends was afflicted by it.

If you earnestly desire to exit the road leading to daily explosions and on the road to parent paradise, you must begin to look at your children with more belief. See their potential more and their child behavior issues and disorders less.

Your child needs you to step up and be their leader in all areas. If it's ADHD you're working with, your child requires the life skills of focus and self-control. Are you with us here? After everything we've shared with you, you should be nodding your head in agreement and chomping at the bit for the "how." We're almost there!

We know that only 1,500 years ago, society believed that the earth was flat. This just proves that beliefs based on other people's thoughts, in a textbook or not, are not always accurate. If you require a little more convincing, allow me to ask you a few questions.

Galatians 5:22-23

But the fruit of the Spirit is love, joy, peace, forbearance, kindness, goodness, faithfulness, 23 gentlenesses and self-control. Against such things, there is no law.

If you had to choose one:
- Is the feeling of anger a good or bad feeling?
- Are frustration and stress good or bad feelings?
- Is believing in defiant children and mental disorders a good or bad belief?

Do you believe we are meant to live in a dark, toxic and life-sucking environment with our children? Do we need just to accept that our teenagers are walking into high schools with a gun — mainly in the USA, but also in countries all over the globe, including Germany, Netherlands and Canada — and killing their classmates before taking their own lives?

Thomas and I were volunteering at a youth ranch in Michigan several years ago. We were expecting a family who had taken in a special needs foster son who was diagnosed with Asperger's syndrome, ADHD and ODD.

This ten-year-old boy named Aaron was also affected by fetal alcohol syndrome. I've seen x-rays of a brain with FAS. They resemble Swiss cheese. Did you know that when a mother drinks alcohol, she stops brain development for that day, leaving the brain with holes?

Everyone involved could only see Aaron's limitations. We were focused on his potential. The truth is that even a child born with brain development issues can still smile. He might respond differently than another child, but he can still feel desire, happiness and joy.

Mom shared with us at the beginning of their visit: "He gets a little bit overstimulated, so we usually have to put him in a timeout to calm him down." Remember what we shared about Dr. Spock's grandson at the beginning of the book?

As we were talking, Aaron was over visiting the horses. He couldn't reach very far through the fence, so he decided to climb on it. Worried that the old fence would give way under him, mom called out, "Hey, Aaron, get down from the fence." He looked over and hopped off the fence.

A few minutes later, guess what he did? Yep. You guessed it. Aaron climbed back up on the fence. Again Mom yelled out, a little more annoyed this time, "Aaron! Get down!" After a couple more times, Mom warned, "If you keep climbing on the fence, we are going to have a timeout. You just aren't listening."

Aaron needed a goal to help him consciously choose something other than what he habitually did, which was to ignore his mother! I asked Mom if it was all right to go and have a little chat with Aaron. She told me I could but continued to explain that I would be wasting my time.

"That's okay! I have time." I strolled over to Aaron with a big smile on my face with only one purpose. It wasn't to get Aaron to comply; it was to find out what was important to him while visiting the ranch.

"Aaron, what would you like to do here today? Would you like to feed the horses, pet the horses, or ride the horses?" I assumed that he would want to ride the horses. I wouldn't have gotten his attention if I had just offered that to him as a bribe. That's not what he wanted.

"I want to feed the horses!" He was engaged and excited.

"Cool, what will you be feeding them?" After asking a few more validating questions, I discovered what was important to Aaron. He wanted to feed hay to the horses with his hands.

"Okay, Aaron. Let's agree. If your feet stay on the ground from now on, you'll be letting us know you're ready to feed the horses. If your feet end up on the fence, that will let us know you're not that interested in feeding the horses. So, tell me where your feet will be if you'd like to feed the horses?"

"If I want to feed the horses, I'll keep my feet on the ground."

"Where would your feet be if you wanted to stop feeding the horses?"

"On the fence."

All I did was create an environment that allowed Aaron the opportunity to achieve a goal he chose for himself. Mom wasn't scared to voice her opinion. "That might work for five minutes, but he'll forget."

Well, an hour passed, and Aaron's feet never touched the fence. He was cooperative and content all day long! He was even seemingly out of sight from his parents at one point, and he never secretly jumped up on the fence. We could see his feet firmly planted on the ground the entire time.

Aaron was shown what he could do to produce success for himself. We focused on what did work and what was important to him—doing so automatically created a new cause that had a brand new, more cooperative effect.

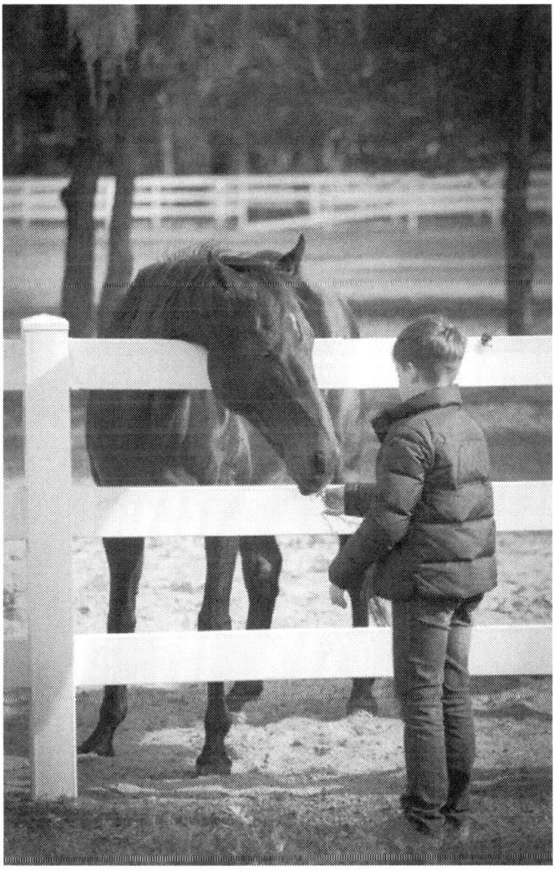

CHAPTER 12

New Beginning

A controlled child without a personal goal to strive for is similar to an animal trapped in a cage.

Can you see that you have all the power? You create the environment you and your children are growing in. Your child's spirit is crying out for more independence, confidence and growth! Make it happen!

A burning desire to be, do and have must fill their hearts until it overflows into action. Your child will choose to cooperate and work with you as a team. You are the only person in the world who can put in the effort necessary to wake up the champion in your child.

Are you as heartbroken as I was to learn that timeouts and takeaways are simply theory and learning that Dr. Spock's grandson committed suicide? We're with you.

I truly believed that psychologists and pediatricians knew what they were doing regarding normal child behavior. I gave them all my power! Doing so set my children up for failure in school and beyond.

It's now easy to see that well-meaning psychologists simply practice on children like guinea pigs hoping for the best. What's the result? Millions of children are being prescribed medication unnecessarily.

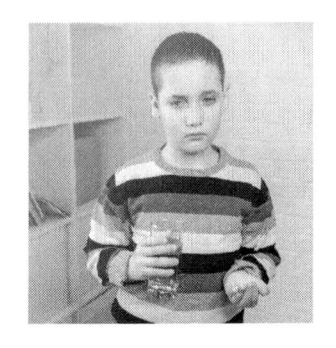

A child controlled by parents without a personal goal is similar to an animal trapped in a cage; they're likely to explode! With more than half of today's children being prescribed medication, it's proof positive they already are!

It's time to step up as parents and take over the bringing up of our children with 100% belief in their capabilities. We must begin to encourage our children to take chances, make mistakes and strive for more! This is the secret to raising outstanding champion kids!

It's time to lift our children, to motivate them to strive to be the best they can be. We need to release the excuses and alibis and develop a list of life skills to teach them.

Perhaps you're like us and agree with Dr. John Locke. He had it right back in the 17th century when he wrote in his renowned *Essay Concerning Human Understanding* that all children are better off guided with love rather than punished with anger. It just makes sense, doesn't it?

After all, they're just a mini-you. They want to be heard. They have a strong desire for independence and to belong socially.

You have 18 years to prepare your kids for life. PERIOD. Motivate them with what's important to them. Maintain integrity by rewarding them precisely what they'd earn if they were in the real world.

You see, raising children with the thought that it's your job to make your kids happy is the wrong foundation. You must realize that the more you give your child, the more they want and the less they desire to do things independently.

You can never fill their void when it comes to authentic happiness. It's up to you to create an environment that will give your children and teenagers purpose, drive and enthusiasm.

Keystone habits are the breeding ground for other smaller practices. Everything you strive for as a parent will fall right into place when you get the formula for an empowering environment correct! You'll end up living the parenting life of your dreams with healthy, happy, cooperative kids and teenagers who eventually become champion adults!

You must know that if you continue on the desperate parenting path you're on, nothing is ever going to change for you or them. Your children will never outgrow temper tantrums, just like they will not grow into knowing how to drive a car.

They require a strong desire to learn a more empowering and happy way to get what they want from you. That's it! You have all the arsenal you need already.

When you look at the tip of an iceberg, you're only seeing a fraction of what exists. All the power is there. It's hidden in the water!

You are at a fork in the road! It's time to decide to turn in the opposite direction from what you are used to.

When you feel anger,
turn toward <u>understanding</u>.

When you feel frustration,
turn toward <u>validation</u>.

When you feel overwhelmed,
turn toward <u>your desires</u>.

Then, make a win-win plan!

Where it all began

Back in 1994, God gave me a dream to find a way to help all children discover their true potential of greatness before the age of 12. Thomas Liotta decided that when he had the chance to teach, he would use the opposite of anything negative with his students, also in 1994.

Thomas Liotta

He created a classroom environment that indeed offered his students free will. His belt advancement tests included life skills like focus, self-control, responsibility and self-discipline. He spent over 15 years working with 1,000s of students. He developed a language and full curriculum of powerful, proactive strategies.

Creating Champions For Life builds self-esteem and pushes kids to choose new, more positive behavior patterns. Your children will have the ability to get what they want in life with love, harmony and acceptance. You'll get to enjoy spending time with amazingly outstanding kids!

I began implementing Thomas' methods in my home. I needed to see for myself if this would work for parents. Of course, it did!

Universal truths are universal.

That means they work for ALL!

Watching my children go from having ADHD and oppositional defiant disorder diagnoses to healthy, happy, cooperative kids was like witnessing a miracle! They were blossoming like a bouquet of sun-kissed roses.

They were:
- excited to earn things;
- getting along;
- cooking me breakfast in bed;
- helping without being asked, joyfully;
- grateful;
- respectful;
- happier with a new zest for life; and
- setting goals and working towards them.

I could go on and on with the positive benefits validating and teaching my children brought my family. I was free! No longer did I feel responsible for the results of my children.

If they wanted pizza on Friday night, they made it happen. If they wished for happiness, all they had to do was choose it for themselves!

Since launching our Rapid Growth Parenting program, dozens of other families have transitioned from their dark, toxic and stressful environment to order, peace and harmony as well. We want to help you make the transition too! You can do it! All you have to do is decide! We've got the rest covered.

You now have a strong foundation for understanding your child. Begin making plans to give your children the opportunity to thrive. You know how to change a habit. You know that your child can develop new neural pathways by repeating a specific behavior.

First ... you need a strong "WHY".

Do you know "why" you want to go on a brand new parenting journey filled with laughter, love and joy?

How will your life change when your children work with you in harmony with every request?

How will it affect you spiritually, relationally, mentally?

Once you believe you have the answers to these questions, ask yourself, "Why is this important to me?" Then ask why repeatedly until you feel in your heart that you are ready to take a chance. Continue to explore until you feel excited to make a difference for your children and family.

You see, raising healthy, happy, cooperative kids is a goal. It's a great goal. But, unless you have your "why" big enough, you won't have the power to persist through obstacles in the beginning when things seem difficult and slow.

Do you have why you're choosing to make a positive transformation with your child written out? If not, do that and then come back to this page. It's just you and your thoughts. We realize that no one will know if you took the time to do this exercise.

Find your "why"; find your strength!

Okay! Got it? Great! We invite you to join the Creating Champions for life Parent Infantry!

We see Creating Champions For Life expanding to the following areas:
- Daycare centers;
- Private schools;
- Life skills training centers;
- Summer camps;
- After-school programs;
- Workshops and seminars;
- Churches; and
- More.

We are looking to develop CCFL coaches, mentors, and leaders to effectively work with parents and children globally. Whatever you see for yourself, it all begins with mastering proactive child-rearing skills!

Congratulations for reading all the way to the end! Excellent parenting! Now you are ready for an authentic transformation in your family.

"Here's to your PARENTING SUCCESS!"

Do you need help now? Please visit:

https://learntospeakkid.com.

Made in the USA
Columbia, SC
26 September 2023